A Night the Stars
Danced for Joy

For Erin and Leigh

A NIGHT THE STARS
DANCED FOR JOY

Bob Hartman
Illustrations by Tim Jonke

The shepherd, the shepherd's wife and the shepherd boy lay on their backs on top of the hill.

Their hands were folded behind their heads, and their feet stretched out in three directions like points on a compass. Their day's work was done. Their sheep had dropped off to sleep. And they had run out of things to say.

So they just lay there on top of that hill and stared lazily into the night sky.

It was a clear night. There were no clouds for shy stars to hide behind. And the bolder stars? For some reason, they seemed to be shining more proudly than any of the shepherds could remember.

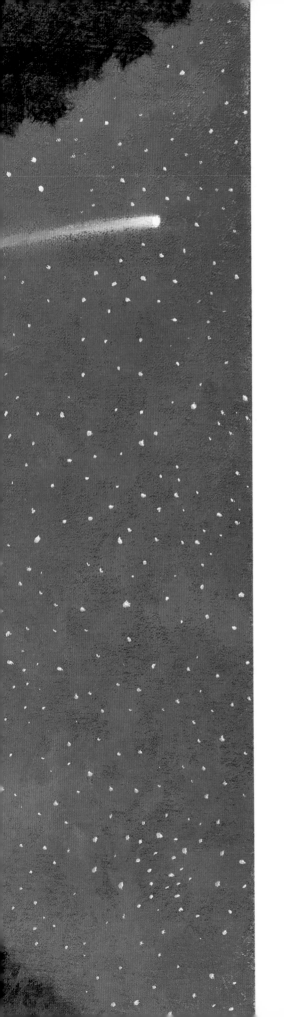

Suddenly, what must have been the boldest star of all came rushing across the sky, dancing from one horizon to the other and showing off its sparkling serpent's tail.

"Shooting star," said the boy dreamily. "Make a wish."

The shepherd and his wife said nothing. They were too old for games and too tired tonight, even to say so.

But they were not too old for wishing.

The shepherd fixed his eyes on a cluster of stars that looked like a great bear. And he thought about the cluster of scars on his leg— jagged reminders of a battle he'd fought with a real bear long ago. A battle to save his sheep.

There were other scars, too, mapped out like a hundred roads across his back. Souvenirs of his battles with that Great Bear, Rome. The land of Israel belonged to his people, not to the Roman invaders. So why should he bow politely to their soldiers and surrender his sheep for their banquets? Greedy tyrants. Uniformed thieves. That's what they were. And even their claw-sharp whips would not change his mind.

And so the shepherd made a silent wish. He wished for someone to save him. From violence. From greed. From bears.

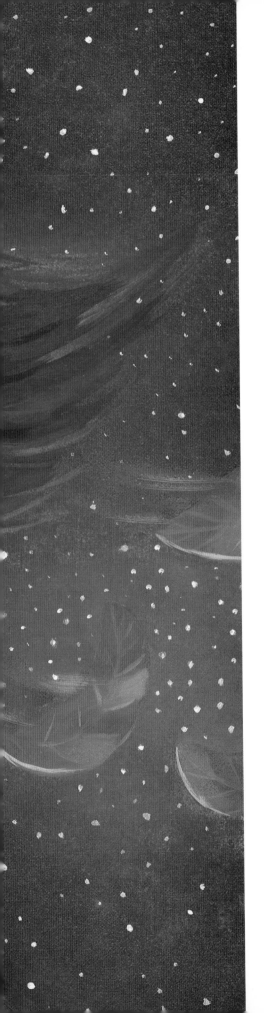

The shepherd's wife had her eyes shut. This was the hardest time of the day for her. The time when there was nothing to do but try to fall asleep. The time when the wind always carried voices back to her. Her voice and her mother's. Angry, bitter voices. Voices hurling words that hurt. Words she wished she'd never spoken. Words she couldn't take back now, because her mother was dead. And there was no chance to say she was sorry.

And so the shepherd's wife made a silent wish, too. She wished for peace, for an end to those bitter voices on the wind.

The shepherd boy grew tired of waiting.
"All right," he said finally.
"*I'll* make a wish then. I wish... I wish... I wish something interesting would happen for a change. Something exciting. I'm tired of just sitting on this hill night after night. I want something to laugh about. To sing and dance about."

The shepherd turned to look at his wife.

The shepherd's wife opened her eyes and shook her head.

But before either of them could say anything, something happened. Something that suggested the shepherd boy just might get his wish.

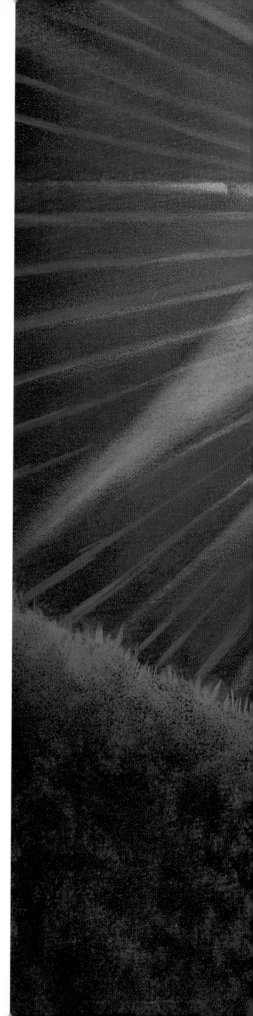

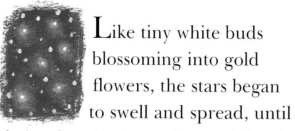Like tiny white buds blossoming into gold flowers, the stars began to swell and spread, until their edges bled together and the sky was filled with a glowing blanket of light. And then that blanket of light began to shrink and gather itself into a brilliant, blinding ball that hung above them.

 The shepherds dared
not move. All they
could do was stare
into that light. They
watched it slowly
change again. Shining
rays stretched into arms. Legs kicked
out like white beams. And a glowing
face blinked bright and burning.
The light sprouted wings. It took
the shape of an angel. And it spoke.

"Don't be afraid," the angel said.
"But sing and dance for joy! I have
good news for you. Today, in
Bethlehem, your Savior was born—
the special one whom God promised
to send you. Here's the proof: if you
go to Bethlehem, you will find the
baby wrapped in cloths and lying in
a feed trough."

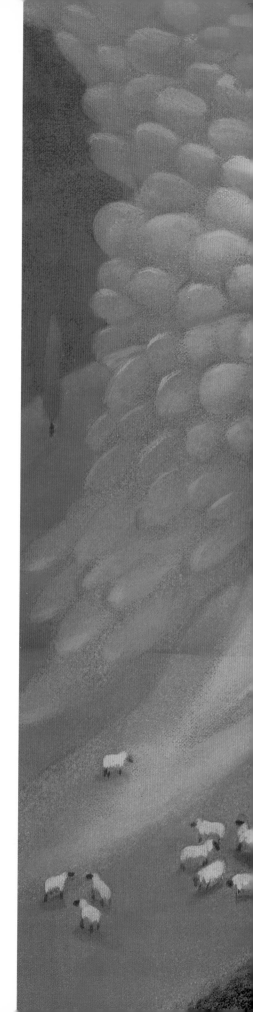

 The shepherds were still too shocked to speak. But that didn't keep them from thinking.

"Don't be afraid?" thought the shepherd. "He's got to be joking."

"A baby in a feed trough?" thought the shepherd's wife. "Why even our own son got better treatment than that."

"Sing and dance for joy?" thought the shepherd boy. "Now that's more like it!"

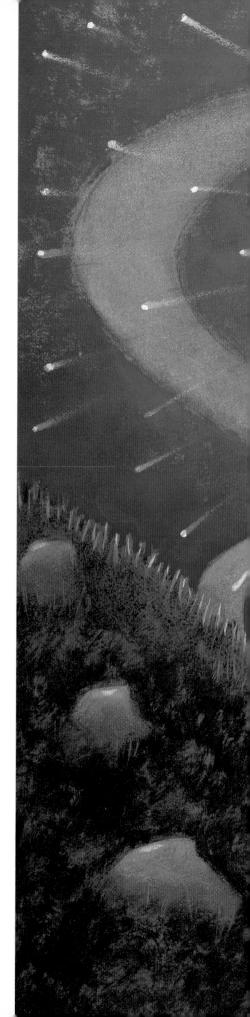

 And, as if in answer to the boy's thought, the angel threw his arms and legs wide, like the first step in some heavenly jig.

But instead, he flung himself—could it be?—into a thousand different pieces of light, pieces that scattered themselves across the dark blue of the night and landed where the stars had been. Pieces that turned into angels themselves, singing a song that the shepherds had never heard before, to a tune that had been humming in their heads forever.

"Glory to God in the highest!" the angels sang. "And peace on earth to all."

Some plucked at lyres. Some blew trumpets. Some beat drums. Some banged cymbals. There were dancers, as well— spinning and whirling, larking and leaping across the face of the midnight moon.

Finally, when the music could get no louder, when the singers could sing no stronger, when the dancers could leap no higher, when the shepherds' mouths and eyes could open no further, everything came to a stop.

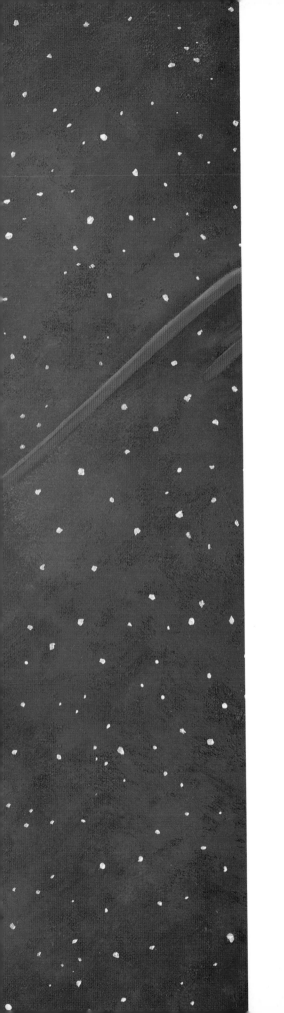

As quickly as the angels had come, they were gone. The sky was silent and filled once more with twinkling stars. The shepherds lay there for a moment, blinking and rubbing their eyes.

At last the shepherd struggled to his feet. "Well," he said, "looks like we'd better find this baby."

The shepherd's wife pulled herself up, shook the grass off her robe and ran her fingers absently through her hair.

The shepherd boy leaped eagerly to his feet and shouted "Hooray!"

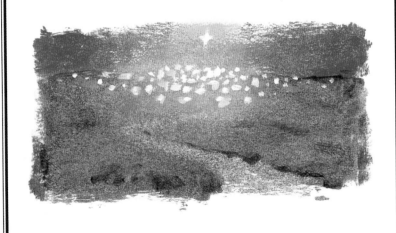

When they got to Bethlehem, things were just as the angel had said. A husband and a young mother. And a baby in a feed trough. A family much like the shepherd's, in fact. Was it possible, the shepherd wondered, for one so small, so poor, so ordinary, to the be the Savior? The Promised One?

Then the shepherd told the young mother about the angels. And that's when he knew. It was the look in her eyes. The look that said, "How wonderful!" but also, "I'm not surprised." There was something special going on here. The angels knew it. The mother knew it. And now the shepherd and his family knew it, too.

"Well," said the boy as they made their way back to the hill, "my wish came true. Too bad you didn't make a wish."

The shepherd said nothing. But he ran one finger gently along his scars. Was he imagining things, or were they smaller now?

The shepherd's wife said nothing. She was listening. There were no bitter voices on the wind now. There were songs—heaven songs—and the cry of a newborn child.

"Glory to God in the highest!" she shouted suddenly.

"And peace to everyone on earth!" the shepherd shouted back.

Then the shepherd boy shouted, too—"Hooray!"—and danced like an angel for joy.

Text copyright © 1993 Bob Hartman
Illustrations copyright © 1996 Tim Jonke
This edition copyright © 1996 Lion Publishing

The moral rights of the author and artist
have been asserted

Published by
Lion Publishing plc
4050 Lee Vance View, Colorado Springs,
CO 80918, USA
ISBN 0 7459 3684 9

First edition 1996
10 9 8 7 6 5 4 3 2 1 0

This story first appeared in *Angels, Angels All Around*,
published by Lion Publishing

Library of Congress CIP data applied for

Printed and bound in Singapore